Fetishists

Adrian Collins

Adrian Collins

Copyright Page

Index

How They Are Formed

Fetishes are formed from a complex combination of personal experiences, psychological associations and external stimuli. To understand how they are created, it is important to consider that our brain functions as a storehouse of memories and sensations, where each experience can leave a mark. From an early age, we are susceptible to associating certain objects, situations or stimuli with emotions, whether it be pleasure, curiosity or even surprise. These associations can become stronger over time, especially if they are repeated in meaningful or intense contexts.

A typical example is when a small child accidentally experiences a moment that combines something unusual with strong emotions. It may be a texture, such as leather or silk, that in a moment of vulnerability or excitement is perceived as something pleasurable. Although at the time the child does not understand what is happening, the child's brain registers the sensation as something positive. Later, that object or situation can revive those emotions and become a point of attraction, although the person is not always aware of why.

Curiosity also plays a role. Fetishes often develop because something unexpectedly catches our attention and sparks an interest that intensifies over time. For example, if someone grows up seeing specific images or situations in the media, such as high heels in glamorous scenes, their brain may associate those elements with sensuality or power. This doesn't happen instantly; it's a gradual process that is reinforced by exposure and repetition.

Another essential factor is the emotional context in which an experience occurs. Intense emotions, whether positive or negative, can cause certain things to become deeply imprinted in our minds. For example, if someone has a moment of strong emotional connection with another person while a particular stimulus is present, such as a smell, a piece of clothing, or a sound, their brain can link that stimulus with the feeling of intimacy. Over time, that element becomes a trigger for reviving that emotional connection, transforming into a fetish.

Furthermore, the human brain is naturally creative and looks for ways to keep us interested and stimulated. This means that fetishes are often born from a mix of curiosity, exploration, and the need to experience something new. The repetition of certain fantasies or thoughts also reinforces the associated neural connections, making those ideas become more persistent and meaningful.

Early sexual experiences often have a special impact on the formation of fetishes. During these times, the brain is especially sensitive to associating external stimuli with pleasurable sensations. If an object or situation is present in that context, it can become linked to pleasure in a lasting way. This explains why some fetishes seem to arise from seemingly simple or unimportant situations.

Cultural influence should not be underestimated. We live in a world where messages about the body, desire, and objects are present in almost everything we consume. Movies, advertising, and social media can create associations in our minds between certain elements and the idea of attractiveness or desire. While these influences do not always create fetishes on their own, they can be a trigger when combined with personal experiences.

Finally, it should be mentioned that the human mind is deeply unique. What may become a fetish for one person may be completely irrelevant to another. This is due to differences in our life histories, personalities, and how we process experiences. Although some fetishes are more common because they are related to universal stimuli, such as touch or certain scents, many others are deeply personal and reflect the particularities of each individual.

In short, fetishes are formed through a combination of personal experiences, emotional associations, and external stimuli that are uniquely imprinted on our minds. It is a process that can be unconscious, gradual, and in many cases fascinating, because it reveals how our minds transform the everyday into something loaded with meaning. Knowing these mechanisms not only helps us understand ourselves better, but also invites us to accept the diversity of human desires as a natural part of experience.

The Science Behind Desire

Desire is a powerful force that guides many of our decisions and behaviors. From a scientific standpoint, desire is a combination of chemical, neurological, and psychological processes that work together to create that feeling of attraction or need toward something or someone. Although it may seem like something magical or inexplicable, the science behind desire is fascinating and helps us understand why we are drawn to certain things or people.

It all starts in the brain, which is the control center for our emotions and sensations. When something grabs our attention in a special way, certain areas of the brain are activated. One of the most important is the reward system, a network of neurons that includes structures such as the nucleus accumbens, the ventral tegmental area, and the amygdala. This system is designed to motivate us to seek out pleasurable experiences and avoid those that make us uncomfortable. When something attracts us, the reward system releases dopamine, a neurotransmitter known as the pleasure chemical, which makes us feel good and reinforces our interest.

Dopamine plays a key role in desire because it acts as an incentive. When the brain releases dopamine in response to an attractive stimulus, we feel motivated to approach that stimulus or repeat the experience that generated it. For example, if someone feels desire for a specific object, such as a pair of heels, it is because their brain has associated that object with pleasure or satisfaction, releasing dopamine every time they see or imagine it.

Another important chemical in desire is oxytocin, known as the love hormone. Although it is primarily associated with emotional bonding, it also has an impact on physical and emotional desire. When we are around someone we are attracted to or in a situation we find stimulating, the body releases oxytocin, creating a feeling of connection and trust. This combination of dopamine and oxytocin is what makes desire feel so intense and sometimes hard to ignore.

Desire is not only influenced by chemicals in the brain, but also by our previous experiences and our imagination. The associations we have formed throughout life play a major role. For example, if a person has had positive experiences related to a particular stimulus, their brain will remember those experiences and reinforce the desire for that stimulus. Imagination also contributes, as the brain has the ability to create scenarios in which a desire becomes more exciting or attractive.

In addition, social and cultural context influences desire. Our perception of what is desirable or attractive is not formed in a vacuum. It is shaped by our culture, our relationships, and the messages we receive from our environment. The media, for example, has a huge impact on what people find attractive, as it presents images and messages that associate certain objects, behaviors, or appearances with desire and success.

Another fascinating aspect of desire is its relationship to anticipation. The human brain is wired to enjoy not just the outcome of something desired, but also the expectation. This is why the anticipation of an exciting moment, such as a date or special encounter, can be just as pleasurable as the event itself. The brain releases dopamine even as we imagine what is to come, keeping us motivated and excited.

Although desire is a natural experience, it can vary from person to person. Some people are more sensitive to desire cues because their brains release more dopamine in response to certain stimuli. Others experience desire more emotionally than physically, depending on how their brains process the connections between pleasure, memory, and emotion.

In short, desire is the result of a delicate balance between brain chemistry, past experiences, cultural environment, and imagination. Understanding how desire works not only helps us understand our own emotions, but also allows us to appreciate the complexity and richness of human connections. Desire is not just a drive; it is a window into the way our brains motivate us, connect us, and drive us to seek meaningful experiences.

What is a Fetish and What is Not?

A fetish is an intense and specific attraction to an object, body part, situation, or stimulus that, on its own, arouses emotional interest or excitement. This means that, for someone with a fetish, that item has a special meaning that goes beyond what most people might perceive. For example, a pair of high heels is not just a fashion accessory; for someone with a fetish, it can be a direct source of desire or a crucial part of their fantasies.

What distinguishes a fetish from other forms of attraction or preference is the intensity of the emotional and psychological connection to that item. While many people may find certain objects or details attractive, a fetish implies that that item becomes almost indispensable to generating interest or pleasure. It is not simply a taste; it is a psychological need that adds special value to that object or situation. For example, someone might prefer a certain item of underwear on a partner, but a person with a fetish for that specific item of clothing might consider it the focus of their desire.

A common mistake is to think that anything we really like or are attracted to is automatically a fetish, but this is not true. A preference is simply an inclination toward something that we find attractive or interesting, but it is not indispensable to our desire or enjoyment. For example, preferring people with curly hair is not a fetish; it is an aesthetic preference. On the other hand, if curly hair becomes a necessary element for arousal or pleasure, then it could be considered a fetish.

Fetishes can vary widely in nature. Some are very common, such as those involving feet, while others are more specific, such as an attraction to materials such as latex or leather. The important thing is that the fetish does not always have to be related to something typically considered "sexy" by society. In fact, some fetishes may seem strange or unusual because they are tied to unique personal associations. These associations are often formed throughout life through experiences, emotions, and learning, as we have already explained in previous chapters.

A fetish is also not the same as a fantasy. Fantasies are creative imaginings that we use to explore different forms of desire, but they are not always necessary to feel pleasure in reality. For example, someone may fantasize about a romantic beach scenario, but they don't need to be on a beach to enjoy their relationship. In contrast, a fetish has a more concrete, tangible component; the presence of the object or stimulus in question may be essential to the experience of pleasure.

It's important to clarify that having a fetish is not a bad or strange thing. It is simply an expression of how our brain associates pleasure with certain stimuli. However, not all intense interests are fetishes. For something to be considered a fetish, it must have a clear impact on desire and be recurrently present in thoughts or experiences. For example, enjoying the smell of a specific perfume is not a fetish unless that perfume is necessary to spark interest or generate an intense emotional response.

Furthermore, a fetish doesn't always have to do with anything sexual. While it's most often associated with physical desire, it can also be related to the emotional or mental pleasure someone feels when interacting with the object or situation in question. For example, some people may have a fetish for certain sounds or textures because they bring them a sense of calm or happiness.

Finally, it is crucial to understand that fetishes, although they may seem unusual to those who do not have them, are a natural part of human diversity. What for one person is just an insignificant detail, for another can be a source of joy or fascination. The key to identifying a fetish is in the intensity, recurrence and need for that stimulus to experience a specific feeling of pleasure or attraction.

In short, a fetish is a unique and powerful connection to something that has special meaning for the person experiencing it. It is not simply a taste or preference, but a deep psychological and emotional bond that influences desire. Knowing how to distinguish between a fetish and other types of attraction helps us better understand our own and others' emotions, embracing the diversity of ways people find pleasure and meaning in their lives.

Adrian Collins

Cultural and Social Factors in the Creation of Fetishes

Cultural and social factors play a huge role in the creation and development of fetishes. Although fetishes may seem personal and intimate, they do not arise in isolation. We are constantly influenced by the environment we live in, the norms of our society, the images we see in the media, and the shared experiences within our communities. All of these contribute to how we perceive the world, what we find attractive, and how our desires are shaped.

Firstly, the culture we grow up in has a direct impact on what we associate with attractiveness or pleasure. Every society has its own beauty standards, ideals and taboos. For example, in some cultures, wearing tight clothing or specific accessories is highly valued, which can create a special attraction to these items in some people. Similarly, there are cultures where certain parts of the body, such as the feet or hands, are seen as particularly sensual, while in others they have no special connotation at all. These cultural associations can sow the seed for the formation of fetishes, as our brains learn to relate certain stimuli with desire or interest.

The media also plays a huge role in this process. From movies and TV shows to advertisements and social media, we are constantly exposed to images that reinforce certain ideals or patterns of attraction. For example, if a person wearing glasses is always portrayed in the media as mysterious or intellectual, some people may develop a special interest in glasses as a symbol of attraction. Similarly, certain objects or materials, such as leather or lace, can take on special meaning when repeatedly associated with scenes of romance or desire on screen.

Another important social factor is the impact of norms and taboos. Often, what is considered forbidden or out of the ordinary in a society can become more attractive precisely because of its transgressive nature. This phenomenon has to do with how our brain works: what is less accessible or more mysterious tends to arouse more curiosity and interest. For example, in societies where showing certain parts of the body is very restricted, those same areas can become the focus of fetishes. What is forbidden is often associated with what is exciting, which reinforces the attraction to certain elements.

Social experiences also greatly influence the formation of fetishes. From an early age, we interact with other people who pass on their own ideas, tastes, and values to us. These interactions can leave deep impressions on us that are later reflected in our desires. For example, if someone is constantly complimented for wearing a specific type of clothing or accessory, they may begin to associate that item with positive feelings, which could potentially develop into a fetish over time. Similarly, a meaningful experience, such as a romantic event involving a particular place or object, can leave an emotional mark that influences future preferences.

It is important to mention that social changes also impact the way fetishes are formed. Trends in fashion, technology and entertainment can introduce new stimuli that were not so relevant before. For example, the rise of video games and cosplay has led to certain costumes or characters now being a focus of attraction for many people. The same occurs with social networks, where certain styles or aesthetics become popular and can influence the tastes of the new generations.

Furthermore, social norms about what is or is not acceptable in terms of desire also shape how fetishes are expressed. In some more open societies, people may feel more comfortable exploring their interests, while in more conservative societies, fetishes may develop more covertly, as a way of dealing with repression or stigma. This demonstrates how the social environment not only influences which fetishes are developed, but also how people relate to them.

Finally, it is crucial to understand that fetishes are not formed solely by external factors. There is always an interaction between what we absorb from the environment and our own personal experiences and characteristics. However, cultural and social factors provide a framework that shapes our ideas of attraction and desire, creating fertile ground for fetishes to flourish.

In conclusion, the culture and society we live in act as a mirror that reflects and reinforces certain patterns of desire. From cultural norms and media images to social experiences and generational shifts, these factors influence how fetishes are formed and how we relate to them. Understanding this context helps us appreciate the diversity and complexity of the ways people experience desire, reminding us that our preferences are deeply connected to the world around us.

The Psychology of Secrecy and Fetish Shame

The psychology of secrecy and shame related to fetishes is a complex topic that is deeply connected to how people perceive themselves and how they believe they will be judged by others. For many people, fetishes are an intimate part of their identity that they prefer to keep hidden, either out of fear of rejection, judgment, or simply the discomfort of sharing something so personal. This secrecy can be both an emotional burden and a source of internal contradictions, as what brings them pleasure can also be a cause of worry or conflict.

Secrecy around fetishes doesn't just come out of nowhere. It's influenced by social norms, cultural values, and in many cases, religious or moral beliefs. In societies where sex and sexuality are considered taboo subjects, speaking openly about desires that are considered unconventional can be especially difficult. The idea that something is "weird" or "wrong" creates a sense of isolation, as if the person is the only one in the world with those feelings. This isolation, in turn, reinforces the secrecy, creating a cycle that's hard to break.

Shame is another important component in this dynamic. Many people with fetishes may experience an internal struggle between what they are attracted to and what they believe they should be attracted to based on societal norms. This conflict can lead to feelings of guilt or discomfort, especially if they have received negative messages about their sexuality in the past. For example, someone who grew up in an environment where certain desires or behaviors were ridiculed may internalize those judgments and feel like something is "wrong" with them.

Shame is also closely linked to the fear of rejection. Sharing a fetish with a partner or friends can be scary because it involves opening up in a very vulnerable way. Many people fear being seen as abnormal, perverse, or undesirable, which can lead them to hide this part of themselves even in close relationships. This fear is not unfounded, as others' reactions can range from acceptance and curiosity to judgment or ridicule.

It's important to note that not all people feel shame about their fetishes, but for those who do, the effects can be significant. Prolonged shame can lead to emotional problems such as anxiety, low self-esteem, or even depression. It can also affect relationships, as keeping important secrets can create emotional distance between people. In some cases, the stress associated with the secret can even cause the fetish to take up a disproportionate amount of space in a person's life, becoming an obsession or a constant source of worry.

Secrecy, on the other hand, is not always seen as a negative thing by those with fetishes. For some people, keeping their desires private can be a way of protecting something they consider special or sacred. Secrecy can add an element of mystery and exclusivity that heightens the experience. However, this type of secrecy is different from that based on shame. When secrecy is chosen out of pleasure rather than fear, it can be a source of satisfaction rather than stress.

The psychology of secrecy and shame also has evolutionary roots. As social beings, humans are designed to seek acceptance in their communities, as acceptance is essential for survival. Anything that makes us feel different or apart can trigger an internal alarm that drives us to hide those aspects of ourselves. In the case of fetishes, the desire to fit in can clash with the need to express oneself, creating an internal tension that is difficult to resolve.

One of the keys to overcoming this shame is to understand that fetishes are a natural part of human diversity. They are not something one deliberately chooses, but rather arise from a combination of experiences, emotional associations, and individual characteristics. Recognizing this can help people accept themselves and see their desires not as something "bad," but as a unique expression of their personality.

Opening up to someone you trust can also be an important step in easing the burden of secrecy and shame. Talking about a fetish in a safe, non-judgmental environment can help normalize the experience and reduce isolation. However, not everyone is ready for this step, and that's okay too. The important thing is for each person to find a balance between their need for privacy and their desire to feel authentic and accepted.

In summary, secrecy and shame related to fetishes are the result of a complex interaction between social, cultural, and personal factors. While secrecy can be a way to protect oneself from judgment, it can also become an emotional burden if it is driven by shame. Personal acceptance, understanding that fetishes are a natural part of human psychology, and the support of safe and supportive relationships are key tools for dealing with these emotions and living a fuller, more authentic life.

From the Common to the Unusual

The world of fetishes encompasses such a wide variety, ranging from what many people might consider common to what may seem unusual or even surprising. This range of preferences shows how diverse and unique the human mind is. Understanding this variety helps us appreciate that fetishes are not an isolated oddity, but rather an expression of how each person connects their desire with specific emotions, experiences, and stimuli.

When we talk about common fetishes, we are referring to those that are, in some way, more present in the collective imagination and that many people have come to consider as part of what is accepted or expected. For example, the attraction to certain types of clothing such as lingerie, high heels or uniforms is something that appears frequently in different cultures. These fetishes are usually influenced by the media, fashion and cultural standards that associate these elements with sensuality, power or sophistication. We can also include in this category the preference for parts of the body that are traditionally considered attractive, such as feet, hands or hair.

Although not everyone shares these attractions, they are common enough for many people to recognize them without being surprised.

However, when we move into the unusual, we find a wide range of fetishes that may be less well-known or simply not discussed as often. This is where preferences that some people find surprising or out of the ordinary come into play. For example, there are those who find pleasure in specific textures, such as leather, latex, or velvet, not just because of how they look, but because of how they feel to the touch. Others may be drawn to objects or items that don't have a direct connection to sexuality, such as balloons, specific toys, or even certain types of food. These less conventional interests are often a reflection of very personal experiences or unique associations that each individual has developed throughout their life.

It is important to understand that the distinction between common and unusual does not imply a value judgment. What may be completely normal for one person may be something they have never considered for another. The perception of what is common or rare is also influenced by cultural and generational factors. For example, in a more conservative era, certain tastes that are now considered acceptable were seen as taboo. Similarly, fetishes that were once considered unusual have gained visibility thanks to the internet and communities that have found safe spaces to share their interests.

Another thing that influences this perception is how many people are willing to openly talk about their preferences. In general, it's easier for someone to share a fetish that they know others also have, such as an attraction to lingerie. Conversely, when a person feels that their interest is very specific or unique, they may prefer to keep it a secret for fear of judgment or rejection. This doesn't mean that these less common fetishes are necessarily rare; often, they just aren't talked about as much as others.

Unusual fetishes can also be related to emotional associations or significant events in a person's life. For example, someone who had a positive or intense experience related to a specific object may develop an emotional connection that later develops into a fetish. This demonstrates how our desires are deeply influenced by our personal histories and how what we are drawn to is not always something we can easily explain or make sense to others.

An interesting point is that, although some fetishes may seem unusual at first glance, they have logical explanations from a psychological point of view. For example, the attraction to inanimate objects, such as shoes or gloves, may be due to how these objects symbolize something else, such as elegance, power or mystery. In other cases, the pleasure may simply come from the sensory stimulation that these items produce, whether due to their texture, shape or even their smell.

As we explore this variety, it's important to maintain an open and understanding attitude. All fetishes, from the most common to the most unusual, are expressions of human diversity and should not be a cause for shame or ridicule. Understanding this breadth helps us see that there is no "right" way to experience desire and that what matters is how each person finds satisfaction and connection with their own interests.

In conclusion, fetishes span a spectrum as wide as human experiences themselves. From those that are more common and accepted to those that are less conventional, they all have a reason for being and reflect the complexity of our minds and emotions. Instead of classifying them as normal or weird, the most valuable thing we can do is recognize them as part of what makes us unique and celebrate the diversity of our ways of feeling and experiencing desire.

Challenges and Benefits

Talking about the challenges and benefits of fetishes involves looking honestly and deeply at how they affect the people who have them. Fetishes, like any aspect of sexuality, can be both a source of pleasure and self-discovery, and a challenge that requires balance and understanding. Although they are a natural part of human diversity, confronting them can bring up personal and social questions, while also offering opportunities for personal growth and connection with others.

One of the main challenges that people with fetishes face is social stigma. Society, in many cases, is not completely open to accepting desires that are considered unconventional or outside of what is expected. This judgment can lead to feelings of shame, isolation, and fear of rejection. People who have fetishes often fear being judged as abnormal or inappropriate, leading them to keep their preferences a secret. This secrecy, while it may protect them from immediate judgment, can also create emotional barriers, even with close people like partners or friends.

Another common challenge is balancing the fetish with daily life. For many people, the fetish is just one part of their sexuality and does not dominate every aspect of their life. However, in some cases, it can become an obsession or something that interferes with healthy relationships or personal responsibilities. For example, if someone feels they need to constantly satisfy their fetish in order to feel happy or complete, this can cause problems in both their emotional well-being and interpersonal relationships. Finding a healthy balance is essential to prevent a desire from becoming a source of stress or conflict.

Furthermore, there is the challenge of sharing this part of oneself with a partner. Talking about a fetish can be a moment of extreme vulnerability, as it involves trusting that the other person will not react with judgment or rejection. Some people fear that their partner will not understand or be willing to participate in their preferences, which can lead to conflict or a feeling of not being fully accepted. On the other hand, not sharing this information can create emotional distance, as an important part of oneself is hidden.

However, fetishes also have significant benefits that often go unnoticed. First, they can be a powerful source of self-knowledge. Exploring a fetish forces people to reflect on what they are truly attracted to and why. This process of introspection can lead to a better understanding of themselves, not only in terms of sexuality, but also how they emotionally connect to the world.

Another important benefit is that fetishes can enrich relationships, as long as they are handled with communication and respect. Sharing a fetish with a partner can be a deeply intimate experience, as it involves a level of openness and trust that strengthens the bond. Additionally, exploring these preferences together can add novelty and excitement to the relationship, creating a deeper and more fulfilling connection.

From a broader perspective, fetishes can also be a tool to challenge societal norms and expectations. By accepting and celebrating their own desire, people with fetishes can contribute to a more inclusive and open society when it comes to sexuality. This process of acceptance can inspire others to be more authentic and less afraid of what makes them unique.

It's important to note that although fetishes may seem complicated or difficult to handle at first, many of the challenges associated with them are solvable. Open communication, both with oneself and with others, is key to overcoming stigma and misunderstandings. Seeking reliable information, and if necessary, professional support, can make a huge difference in how someone experiences a fetish.

In short, fetishes present a mix of challenges and benefits that reflect the complexity of the human experience. They can be a source of enjoyment, personal growth, and connection, but they can also pose challenges related to stigma, acceptance, and balance. What is most important is that each person finds their own way to integrate this part of themselves in a way that is healthy and enriching. With understanding and support, fetishes can cease to be a complicated secret and become a natural and valuable expression of who we are.

Fetishistic Psychopathology

Fetish psychopathology is a topic that addresses when fetishes, which are generally a healthy and natural part of human sexual diversity, can become a source of distress or interfere with a person's life. Not all fetishes are problematic, but in certain cases, they can enter a realm where they negatively affect mental health, relationships, and daily functioning. Understanding when a fetish crosses this line is critical to addressing these situations sensitively and seeking appropriate help.

Generally speaking, a fetish is considered part of psychopathology when it meets certain criteria. First, if it becomes an obsession that dominates a person's thoughts, emotions, and behavior, to the point that they neglect other important areas of their life. For example, if someone spends so much time looking for ways to satisfy their fetish that they neglect their job, studies, or relationships, this may be a sign that they need support.

Another indicator is when the fetish causes significant distress. This can take many forms, from feelings of shame and guilt that consume the person, to the inability to enjoy sexual intimacy without the presence of the fetish-related object or stimulus. In some cases, people may feel like they are trapped in a cycle they cannot break, which affects their self-esteem and emotional well-being.

Additionally, a fetish can become a problem when it interferes with consent or respect for others. For example, if someone feels the need to act on their fetish in ways that encroach on another person's boundaries or violate social norms, this can lead to legal, ethical, and relational issues. This type of behavior not only affects the person experiencing it, but also those around them, creating an environment of distrust or discomfort.

From a psychological point of view, fetish-related problems are often connected to deeper factors. Some people develop a problematic relationship with their fetish due to unresolved traumas, experiences of rejection, or a general lack of acceptance of their own sexuality. In these cases, the fetish may be an escape mechanism or a way to deal with difficult emotions, but over time, it can become an additional source of stress.

It is important to mention that not all fetishes related to psychopathology are extreme or rare. Even the most common preferences can be problematic if they become an exclusive need or if they generate internal conflicts. This reinforces the idea that it is not the fetish itself that determines whether it is healthy or not, but the way it is handled and how it affects the person's life.

To deal with fetish-related issues, the first step is to acknowledge them. Many people are afraid to seek help because they fear being judged or misunderstood. However, talking to a mental health professional can be extremely helpful. Psychologists and therapists are trained to approach these issues with empathy and non-judgment, helping people understand their desires and work toward a more balanced relationship with them.

Treatment may include different approaches, depending on the situation. For example, cognitive behavioral therapy can help people identify patterns of thinking and behavior that contribute to the problem and develop strategies to manage them. In cases where there is underlying trauma, trauma-focused therapy may be key to addressing the emotional roots of the fetish.

In some cases, it can also be helpful to work on accepting and integrating the fetish as a natural part of one's sexual identity, as long as it does not cause harm to the person or others. This may involve learning to communicate one's needs openly and respectfully, finding healthy ways to fulfill desire, and building a balanced life that is not defined solely by the fetish.

In conclusion, fetish psychopathology is not about demonizing fetishes or considering them abnormal by default, but about understanding when and why they can become a problem. With the right approach, it is possible to transform these difficulties into an opportunity for personal growth and improved relationships. Ultimately, the most important thing is to remember that we all have the right to explore our sexuality in a way that is healthy and respectful, both for ourselves and for others.

The Impact of Fetish on Self-Image

The impact of fetishes on self-image is a fascinating and often complicated topic. Self-image is the way a person perceives themselves, including their appearance, their identity, and how they feel about who they are. Fetishes can influence this perception in profound ways, both positive and negative, depending on how each individual experiences and integrates them into their life.

For many people, discovering that they have a fetish can be a moment of self-discovery. This can lead to a deeper connection with their sexual and emotional identity. For example, accepting a fetish and understanding that it is a natural part of oneself can strengthen personal confidence. Knowing what you like, understanding why you are attracted to it, and being able to express it without shame can make you feel more in control of your own life. This type of self-acceptance can improve the relationship you have with yourself, promoting a positive self-image.

However, it's not all that simple. Many people with fetishes struggle with feelings of shame, guilt, or even self-rejection. This is especially true if they grow up in environments where their desire is considered strange, inappropriate, or morally wrong. These feelings can erode self-image, making someone feel defective, abnormal, or unworthy of love and acceptance. In some cases, people try to hide their fetish even from themselves, which can cause internal conflicts and increase insecurity.

Additionally, social and cultural context plays a large role in how a fetish affects self-image. We live in a world where certain norms dictate what is acceptable and what is not. If someone feels like their fetish doesn't fit into those norms, they may begin to perceive themselves as different or out of place. This feeling of not belonging can cause a person to distance themselves from others, which negatively impacts their self-esteem. Feeling judged or misunderstood can cause someone to see themselves through the judgmental eyes of others, which amplifies insecurity.

On the other hand, when a person finds communities or partners who accept and celebrate their fetish, the experience can transform their self-image in positive ways. External validation, especially from like-minded people, can help reduce shame and normalize desires that previously seemed strange or problematic. This external acceptance can be the push someone needs to fully embrace that part of themselves.

It's also important to talk about how fetishes can impact self-image through the body. In some cases, the fetish may be directly related to physical appearance or certain bodily features. For example, someone who has a fetish for certain shapes or styles might develop a more positive perception of their own body if they feel they fit that ideal. However, it's also possible for someone to feel inadequate if they feel they don't meet the standards their own fetish highlights. This can lead to insecurities about appearance, affecting both self-esteem and how they relate to their own body.

In more extreme cases, a fetish can become a source of internal conflict if a person feels they cannot control their desire or if they feel defined solely by it. When someone begins to perceive their identity as being reduced to a single aspect of themselves, their self-image can become limited and unbalanced. This phenomenon is not unique to fetishes, but it may be more pronounced in people who struggle to reconcile their desire with other parts of their life.

A powerful tool for managing the impact of a fetish on self-image is self-acceptance. This involves recognizing that we are all complex, that our sexuality is just one part of who we are, and that there is nothing wrong with having desires that differ from other people's. It also involves being kind to yourself and allowing yourself to explore your own identity without judgment. In this process, it can be helpful to surround yourself with people who are understanding and who fully accept you.

Another key element is communication. Talking about a fetish with someone you trust, whether it's a friend, partner, or therapist, can be a liberating experience. Expressing your thoughts and feelings in a safe space can help you view your fetish more objectively, which contributes to a more balanced and positive self-image.

In summary, the impact of fetishes on self-image is complex and multifaceted. It can be a source of empowerment and self-confidence, but it can also lead to internal conflicts and feelings of insecurity. The most important thing is to understand that fetishes are only one part of your identity and that you have the power to decide how to integrate them into your life. With acceptance, support, and a healthy outlook, it is possible to build a strong, positive self-image that celebrates all parts of who you are.

Fetishes and their Representation in the Media

Fetishes have found a place in the media, although the way they are represented varies widely depending on the context, audience, and goals of those who produce that content. From movies and series to books and social media, fetishes appear explicitly or implicitly, often influenced by cultural taboos and entertainment norms. This representation has a significant impact on how people understand, accept, or reject these desires in society and in themselves.

First, it's important to recognize that fetishes are often portrayed in the media as mysterious, forbidden, or even strange. Many films, for example, have used fetishes to add intrigue or to portray characters in eccentric or enigmatic ways. This approach, while it may be appealing to audiences, tends to reinforce the idea that fetishes are something out of the ordinary, reserved for peculiar people or those with secret lives. While this portrayal may generate curiosity, it also contributes to many people feeling ashamed of their own desires, as the implicit message is that these are weird or inappropriate.

Television series have also tackled fetishes, sometimes in a comedic way, other times with a more serious tone. Comedy shows, in particular, tend to exaggerate fetishes to elicit laughs from audiences, presenting them as ridiculous or out-of-place behavior. While this approach can be entertaining, it runs the risk of trivializing the feelings of those with a fetish, which can increase the stigma surrounding the topic. On the other hand, more serious series have attempted to explore the topic in a more nuanced way, showing characters dealing with their desires in authentic and human ways. This type of representation can be valuable, as it helps to normalize fetishes and promote greater understanding.

In the literary realm, fetishes have also found their place, especially in erotic literature. Books such as contemporary romance novels have popularized certain fetishes by presenting them as part of passionate, consensual relationships. This has helped some desires become more accepted in popular culture. However, literature can also perpetuate stereotypes by focusing on specific fetishes while ignoring or marginalizing others. Additionally, many stories focus solely on the sexual aspect of the fetish, leaving aside the emotional or psychological context, which limits a deeper understanding of the topic.

Social media has opened up new possibilities for fetish representation, allowing people to share their interests more openly and find like-minded communities. On platforms like Instagram, TikTok, or Reddit, it's possible to find content that celebrates different fetishes, from artistic photography to discussions about the topic. This type of representation can be empowering, as it provides a space where people can feel seen and understood. However, there are also risks. Social media tends to simplify or commercialize fetishes, turning them into trends or products rather than exploring them as part of personal identity.

Film and television are not the only mediums where fetishes appear. Music and music videos have also played a role in how fetishes are perceived culturally. Many artists have used fetishistic elements in their performances, from clothing and choreography to lyrics that reference specific desires. This use can be seen as a way to break taboos and normalize certain topics, but it can also lead to criticism for trivializing or overly sexualizing aspects of personal identity.

One of the main criticisms of fetish representation in the media is that it is often aimed at a heterosexual, male audience, which excludes other perspectives and experiences. This reinforces a limited and, in some cases, sexist view of fetishes, ignoring their diversity and complexity. Furthermore, the media tends to focus on fetishes that are visually striking or easy to understand, leaving out those that are more emotional or difficult to represent on screen.

Despite limitations, there are positive examples of representation in media. Some films and series have approached fetishes sensitively, showing characters exploring their desires in a respectful and consensual manner. Not only are these depictions more realistic, but they also help educate the public on the topic, reducing stigma and promoting understanding. This type of content can also be comforting for those with a fetish, as they see their experience reflected in a way that validates their feelings and desires.

In conclusion, the media has enormous power to influence how fetishes are perceived in society. While they often fall into stereotypes or exaggeration, they also have the ability to normalize and educate. For this to happen, it is necessary for content creators to approach the topic more responsibly, showing a variety of experiences and contexts. In the end, balanced representation can help demystify fetishes and foster a more open and understanding culture, where people feel free to explore and embrace their desires without shame or judgment.

The Role of Consent

Consent is one of the most important foundations in any interaction involving fetishes or practices related to them. It is the free, informed, and mutual agreement between people participating in an activity. Without consent, any dynamic becomes harmful and possibly traumatic, even if the original intention was not to cause harm. Talking about consent is not only essential to ensure that experiences are safe, but also to foster more respectful and authentic relationships.

When it comes to fetishes, consent takes on an even more important nuance because you're often entering into territories that can be sensitive or misinterpreted. Fetishes, by their nature, involve specific desires that may not be common to all people. This means that you shouldn't assume that the other person will be okay with it or interested in participating. This is where open dialogue becomes a key tool. Talking about boundaries, expectations, and desires not only establishes safe ground, but it also builds trust between the people involved.

Consent, moreover, should be dynamic and ongoing. It's not something you ask for once and take for granted. During any experience, especially if it involves exploring a fetish, it's essential to pay attention to the other person's verbal and nonverbal cues. A simple "yes" at the beginning doesn't mean the other person is comfortable at all times. Changing your mind is completely valid, and respecting that decision is a sign of emotional maturity and empathy. Ignoring a refusal, whether explicit or implicit, not only breaks trust, but can also cause significant emotional damage.

It's common for conversations about consent to feel awkward. Many people aren't used to openly expressing their desires or setting clear boundaries. However, these conversations don't have to be uncomfortable if they're approached with empathy and respect. Creating a safe space where both parties feel heard and understood is essential for consent to flow naturally. This includes not judging another person's desires, even if they're different from your own. Consent isn't just an act of approval, it's also a reflection of acceptance and validation of the other person's needs.

Another crucial aspect of consent in the context of fetishes is the need for education and clarity. Often, people can feel pressured to say yes for fear of disappointing or being judged. This is not real consent, as it does not come from a place of freedom and comfort. Because of this, it is crucial that both parties fully understand what the practice or activity involves. This includes details such as what is expected of each person, how the activity will be carried out, and what boundaries should not be crossed. An honest, pressure-free conversation helps create an environment where everyone can genuinely and safely participate.

Consent also plays an important role in setting boundaries. Setting clear boundaries is not an act of rejection toward the other person, but rather a way to protect yourself emotionally and physically. Boundaries can be specific and direct, such as saying "I don't want to do this" or "I'm not comfortable with this," or more general, such as preferring that certain things not be discussed.

Respecting these boundaries shows that you value the other person's well-being beyond your own wishes. Furthermore, boundaries can be renegotiated over time, but always with the will and agreement of both parties.

Consent also involves recognizing that each person has a unique emotional and psychological context. Some people may be exploring a fetish for the first time and feel vulnerable or unsure. Others may have had negative experiences in the past that make them more cautious. Being aware of these factors and addressing them with care and patience is part of practicing responsible consent. Listening carefully and with empathy helps build a foundation of trust that enriches any shared experience.

An often overlooked topic is consent within established relationships. Many people believe that consent is implied when you are in a relationship, but this is not true. Even in a long-term relationship, each person has the right to set boundaries and decide what practices they do or do not want to explore. Assuming that emotional closeness equals permanent permission is a mistake that can lead to unnecessary tension and conflict.

In the case of fetishes that involve power dynamics, such as role-playing or dominance and submission, consent becomes the fundamental pillar. These practices require an even higher level of communication and trust. Many couples use tools such as contracts, safe words, or signals to ensure that both parties feel safe at all times. These tools are not a sign of distrust, but rather a way to ensure that consent is always present, even in situations where one of the participants assumes a controlling role.

Ultimately, consent benefits not only the person giving it, but also the person asking for it. Knowing that both parties are in full agreement to participate makes the experience much more enjoyable and meaningful. Consent creates a space where people can be authentic and vulnerable without fear of judgment or rejection. This not only enriches the experience itself, but it also strengthens the emotional connection and intimacy between people.

In short, consent is much more than a formality. It is a practice that reflects respect, care, and empathy towards others. In the context of fetishes, where desires can be complex and sometimes misunderstood, consent ensures that all interactions are safe and respectful. Openly speaking, active listening, and respecting boundaries are essential steps to building positive, meaningful experiences that enrich relationships and self-knowledge.

How to Recognize Your Own Fetishes

Recognizing your own fetishes can be a journey of self-discovery filled with surprises, curiosity, and sometimes self-doubt. Fetishes are a natural part of human sexuality, but they aren't always easy to identify because they're often buried under layers of societal norms, insecurities, or ignorance. Knowing what your own fetishes are not only helps you understand yourself better, but it can also open you up to more authentic and fulfilling experiences in your relationships.

The first step to recognizing your own fetishes is to pay attention to what triggers a particular emotional or physical response in you. This can include things you see in movies, TV shows, books, or even in your own fantasies. For example, if you notice that certain materials like leather, silk, or latex spark your interest beyond the ordinary, this could be a sign. The same goes for specific situations, roles, or power dynamics that you find intriguing or arousing. Paying attention to these responses can be the key to beginning to understand your preferences.

Fantasies are another fertile ground for exploring your fetishes. Often, what we imagine in our minds reflects our deepest desires, even if we don't dare to express them out loud. Allow yourself to reflect on your fantasies without judgment. Ask yourself what aspects of those fantasies you find most exciting. Maybe it's not just the context, but a specific detail, like a type of interaction, a sensation, or an emotion that keeps recurring. These clues can be very revealing in identifying patterns in what you're attracted to.

An important aspect of self-discovery is observing how you react to certain stimuli in your everyday life. Maybe you've always had an inexplicable attraction to feet, heels, uniforms, or symbolic objects, but you've never associated it with a fetish. Paying attention to these small details and accepting that they're a valid part of your experience can help you understand yourself better. Often, fetishes start out as a subtle attraction that only becomes clear when you take the time to analyze it.

Talking to yourself can also be very helpful. Often times, fetishes remain hidden because we mentally block them out of shame, fear of judgment, or lack of information. Take a moment to reflect on your past experiences and ask yourself if there is something that you have always been interested in, but have never fully explored. Maybe there is an experience that you remember vividly because it sparked something in you, even if you didn't know how to interpret it at the time. Revisiting those memories from a place of curiosity can shed a lot of light on your desires.

It's normal to feel some resistance when exploring your own fetishes, especially if you feel that they go against what you consider "normal." It's important to remember here that human sexuality is extremely diverse, and there is no single definition of what is acceptable, as long as the line of consent and respect for others is not crossed. Being honest with yourself and allowing yourself to explore without prejudice is essential to recognizing your fetishes. Often, the biggest obstacle to understanding yourself is not society, but your own internal judgments.

Another effective method for identifying your fetishes is to read about them or seek out information. Traditional sex education often leaves out topics like fetishes, which can lead to confusion or ignorance. Exploring reliable resources, such as books, articles, or online communities, can open your eyes to possibilities you may never have considered. Sometimes, finding out that other people share a similar interest can validate it and help you identify it as a fetish.

Talking to trusted people can also be an eye-opening step. If you have close friends or a partner with whom you can share your thoughts, consider opening up this conversation. Often, verbalizing your ideas and hearing others' perspectives can help you organize your own thoughts and discover things you hadn't considered before. The key here is to choose a safe environment where you feel comfortable being vulnerable.

There's no right or wrong way to discover your fetishes, but it's important to approach this process with patience and self-compassion. You might find that your fetishes are simpler than you expected, or you might be surprised to realize that you have more unusual interests. Whatever the case, accepting your desires as a valid part of yourself is a crucial step toward healthily integrating them into your life.

Finally, it's important to remember that you're not obligated to act on every fetish you discover. Acknowledging a fetish doesn't mean it has to become an active part of your sex life, unless you really want it to be. Some people find satisfaction in simply understanding their desires, while others choose to explore them with a partner or solo. The decision is always yours, and the most important thing is that you feel comfortable with whatever path you choose.

In short, recognizing your own fetishes is a process that requires time, attention, and an open mind. By observing your reactions, reflecting on your fantasies, seeking information, and accepting your desires without judgment, you can begin to understand this part of yourself. Self-knowledge is a powerful tool, and discovering your fetishes can be a way to connect more deeply with who you are and what makes you feel fulfilled.

Arousing Fetishes in Other People

Arousing fetishes in other people can be an intriguing and delicate topic that requires sensitivity, open communication, and a lot of respect. This process is not about manipulating or imposing something on someone, but about exploring together and creating an environment where both can feel comfortable and curious. Fetishes, as part of sexuality, are deeply connected to the mind and emotions, so triggering them in someone else depends on establishing trust, generating interest, and stimulating their imagination.

The first step to awakening a fetish in another person is to understand that not all fetishes are universal. What works for one person may not have the same effect on another. That's why the most effective way is to get to know the person you're interacting with intimately. This means paying attention to their interests, what subtly or obviously attracts them, and how they react to different stimuli. Observe their comments, their gestures, and the way they respond to certain topics or images. Often, people reveal their preferences without realizing it, and this can give you an idea of what direction to explore.

Open and honest communication is key. Talking about desires, curiosities, and boundaries creates an environment where both people feel safe to express what they like or are intrigued by. You can start these conversations casually, asking questions like what they find interesting or what draws them in certain situations. For example, if the topic comes up naturally, you could ask if they've ever felt a special attraction to any specific objects, materials, or dynamics. Not only do these questions open the door to exploration, but they also allow you to understand if the person already has latent fetishes that they may not have consciously explored.

Another important aspect is gradual stimulation. Fetishes don't usually appear suddenly; they often develop through repeated experiences that build positive or arousing associations. For example, if you think someone might find a material like leather or silk attractive, you can subtly introduce it in different contexts, such as suggesting clothing or accessories that feature it. Similarly, if you're exploring roles or power dynamics, you can bring up small interactions that reflect those ideas and observe how they react. The key here is to go slowly and pay attention to how the other person responds, adjusting your actions based on their level of interest or comfort.

Creating a supportive environment is essential to awakening fetishes. This means removing any sense of judgment or pressure and instead fostering an atmosphere of play, curiosity, and mutual enjoyment. Often, fetishes develop in environments where people feel free to experiment without fear of rejection. You can accomplish this by suggesting activities or scenarios that explore themes that might awaken a fetish. For example, if you know someone is intrigued by control or submission dynamics, you can propose a fun experience where these dynamics are explored in a light and respectful way.

It's important to note that imagination plays a crucial role in fetishes. Often, these are aroused more by what is hinted at than what is overtly shown. You can take advantage of this by introducing elements that suggest a fetish without being too explicit. For example, accessories, words, or actions that evoke an idea can be more effective than simply naming the fetish. This approach stimulates the other person's mind and allows them to connect their own emotions or fantasies to the experience.

Positive reinforcement is also a powerful element. If you notice the other person showing interest in a topic or situation related to a fetish, it's important to validate that interest in subtle but clear ways. This can be as simple as expressing shared enthusiasm, making comments that highlight how interesting or attractive they are, or showing appreciation for their openness to exploring something new. This type of validation reinforces the idea that it's safe and enjoyable to explore that path together.

Lastly, it's crucial to respect the other person's boundaries at all times. While it's exciting to explore together, it's also important to remember that not everyone is interested in developing fetishes, and that's perfectly okay. If someone expresses discomfort or a lack of interest, it's essential to respect their decision and not push it. Arousing a fetish in someone else should never be a forced or manipulative experience, but rather a mutual exploration that stems from shared desire and curiosity.

In short, awakening a fetish in another person involves getting to know them deeply, encouraging open communication, introducing stimuli gradually, and creating an environment of trust and play. Imagination, validation, and respect are key ingredients to making this exploration positive and enriching. Each person is unique, and the process of discovering what sparks their interest should be approached with patience, sensitivity, and an open mind. In the end, the most important thing is that both people enjoy the process and feel free to be who they really are.

The Most Common Myths About Fetishes

Myths about fetishes are everywhere, and in many cases, these myths create confusion, shame, and misperceptions about the topic. Over the years, misconceptions have multiplied, fueled by a lack of sexual education, cultural biases, and distorted media representations. To better understand what fetishes are and how they influence people, it is crucial to debunk some of the most common myths.

One of the most common myths is that people with fetishes are weird or abnormal. This belief stems from the stigma that has historically surrounded any topic related to non-traditional sexuality. The reality is that fetishes are much more common than most people think. Many studies have shown that a large number of people have some type of fetish or specific sexual interest. The variety of human preferences is immense, and fetishes are simply one more expression of that diversity. Viewing them as something strange only perpetuates misinformation and makes it difficult for people to talk about their desires openly.

Another widely held myth is that fetishes are always extreme or even dangerous. This couldn't be further from the truth. While some fetishes may seem more unusual than others, most are completely harmless and are performed within consensual boundaries between adults. For example, having a particular interest in materials such as silk or leather, or finding certain clothing or situations attractive, is not dangerous or extreme. It's the lack of consent or irresponsible use that makes any practice a problem, not the fetish itself.

There is also a belief that having a fetish means that something is wrong psychologically. This myth comes from old theories that associated fetishes with mental disorders or deviations. Today, modern psychology recognizes that fetishes, for the most part, are a natural part of human sexuality. They are not indicative of mental problems, as long as they do not interfere negatively with a person's life or relationships. In fact, many people with fetishes have perfectly balanced lives and enjoy healthy relationships.

One myth that can cause a lot of harm is the idea that fetishes are shameful and should be kept secret. This encourages a cycle of silence and self-criticism that can be emotionally draining for those with fetishistic interests. The truth is that there is nothing wrong with having a fetish as long as it is lived with respect for oneself and others. Talking openly about one's desires can be liberating and helps create a more genuine connection with partners, removing the need to hide an important part of one's sexual identity.

Many people believe that fetishes are fixed and unchanging, as if someone who has a fetish has always had it or could never become interested in anything else. However, fetishes can evolve over time, just like other aspects of sexuality. Some fetishes arise from personal or cultural experiences, while others may fade away if they no longer have special meaning. This flexibility shows that fetishes are not rigid or set in stone, but rather a dynamic expression of personality.

Another common myth is that fetishes completely dominate a person's sex life.

Although fetishes can be an important source of pleasure, they are not necessarily the only defining aspect of someone's sexuality. Many people with fetishes also enjoy traditional forms of intimacy and have varied sexual interests. Believing that one fetish is all-consuming is oversimplifying the complexity of the human experience.

Finally, there's the myth that fetishes must always be shared with a partner in order to be valid or satisfying. While sharing can enrich a relationship, many people find personal satisfaction in exploring their fetishes alone, whether through fantasies, reading, art, or any other form of expression. The key is for each person to handle their interests in the way that feels most comfortable and pleasurable to them.

Debunking these myths is essential to fostering a healthier and more open understanding of fetishes. By removing stigma and misinformation, a space is created where people can embrace their desires without guilt or fear, and where relationships can be built on respect and communication. Sexuality is diverse, and recognizing that diversity allows us to live more authentically and well.

Living With your Fetish

Living with a fetish is, above all, a journey towards self-understanding, acceptance and balance. For many people, a fetish is a natural part of their identity, a unique expression of their desires and personality. However, the way each individual lives with their fetish can vary depending on their environment, their relationships and their own perception of what it means to have one. This process is not always easy, but with the right information and an open mind, it can be liberating and empowering.

The first step to living with a fetish is to acknowledge and accept it as a normal part of who you are. Many people spend years fighting their own desires, feeling ashamed or confused. This shame often comes from a lack of information or the stigma society can place on anything that falls outside of what is considered traditional. Recognizing that a fetish does not define your worth as a person and that there is nothing inherently wrong with having one is essential to starting to live fully.

Once you've accepted your fetish, it's important to learn about it. Researching its origins, understanding how it affects your life, and learning about other people's experiences can help you see it in a broader perspective. There are online communities and educational resources where you can explore these topics in a safe and respectful way. Knowing more about your fetish allows you to better integrate it into your life, and it also gives you tools to communicate it to others if you choose to share it.

Communication plays a crucial role when it comes to living with a fetish, especially in the context of a relationship. If you decide to share this part of yourself with someone, it's important to do so from a place of trust and mutual respect. Many people fear being judged or rejected, but the reality is that most partners appreciate honesty and vulnerability. How you present your fetish can make a huge difference. Talking about it as something that's part of you, but doesn't completely define you, can help your partner understand it without feeling intimidated or confused.

It's just as important to respect each other's boundaries. While sharing your fetish can be a liberating act, you should also be prepared that not everyone will feel comfortable participating in it. This doesn't mean there's anything wrong with you or your fetish, it simply reflects the diversity of preferences and boundaries that exist in each person. Finding a middle ground where both feel respected and satisfied is a sign of a healthy relationship.

On a personal level, living with a fetish also involves finding ways to enjoy it in ways that don't negatively interfere with your daily life. For some, this means setting aside specific times to explore it, while for others it may become more naturally integrated into their routine. The important thing is that it doesn't become a source of excessive stress or distraction. Maintaining a balance between your fetish interests and other areas of your life, such as work, friendships, and family, is essential to your overall well-being.

Another key aspect is self-esteem. Many people with fetishes struggle with feelings of guilt or insecurity, especially if they feel their desires are not accepted by society. Learning to love yourself as you are, with your quirks and desires, is a powerful step toward a more fulfilling life. Remember that your fetish is just a part of you, not all of you. You are also your talents, your values, your relationships, and your dreams.

Finally, consider seeking support if at any point you feel that your fetish is becoming a source of distress or conflict. Talking to a sexual therapist can be a very enriching experience, as it will help you better understand your desires and manage any negative emotions that may arise. Therapy is not designed to change you, but to empower you and help you live in harmony with yourself.

Living with a fetish doesn't have to be a burden. With acceptance, awareness, communication, and self-care, you can integrate it into your life in healthy and enriching ways. At the end of the day, we are all a sum of our experiences, interests, and desires, and each of those elements has a place in our personal story. Living with your fetish means learning to accept and celebrate who you are, in all your uniqueness and complexity.